Don't Misunderstand
THE MISSION
Of God's Word

The Key to Success
in Ministry & Life

DR. CHARLES D. MILLER

Copyright ©2023 Dr. Charles Miller
Don't Misunderstand the Mission of God's Word

Paperback ISBN: 9798875829840

Published by:
CoolBird Publishing House
792 Commerce Dr., Ste 104
Alexander City, AL 35010
www.coolbirdstudios.com/publishing
Book cover design: Taminko J. Kelley of CoolBird Publishing House

All rights reserved. No part of this publication may be reproduced, stored in a retrieval system, or transmitted in any form by any means - electronic, mechanical, digital, photocopy, recording, or otherwise-without prior written permission of the author. Please purchase only authorized editions. References have been included in the back of this publication. All Scripture quotations, unless otherwise indicated are taken from the NKJV and the KJV Holy Bible.

Printed in the United States of America

Dedication

I dedicate this book to honor my Lord and Savior, Jesus Christ! God has been my strength and portion for 83 years. I thank God for giving me the wisdom and knowledge to help others understand His POWER! 'For God has not given us a spirit of fear, but of power, and of love, and of a sound mind.' (2 Timothy 1:7) By trusting in God, fear was overshadowed by faith! Lastly, John 15:5-6 KJV states, 'I am the vine, ye are the branches: He that abideth in me, and I in him, the same bringeth forth much fruit: for without me ye can do nothing.' Without God, I could do nothing, and I am forever grateful for His unconditional love.

-Dr. Charles D. Miller

BIO

Dr. Charles D. Miller is the third of five children born to the late Rev. & Mrs. James A. Miller on February 16, 1940. At an early age, he confessed Christ and was baptized at Millspring Baptist Church in Weir, MS. He later joined New Hope Grove M.B. Church in Ridgeland, MS, under the leadership of Rev. Carl Thomas. After joining the body of Christ, Rev. Miller served as a deacon, Sunday School teacher, and member of the New Hope Grove Male Chorus. In 1981, God called him into the ministry, and in 1983, he was called to pastor New Hope Grove. In 1997, the Lord guided his vision, and New Birth Fellowship M.B. Church was born. He has been a faithful pastor for 40 years, still trusting and believing in God. Dr. Miller received his primary education in the Ackerman Public School System in Mississippi and attended Hinds Jr. College, Jackson College of Ministries, and MS Baptist Seminary. He received the Pastor's Alternative for Teaching Certification through the National Baptist Sunday School Publishing Board and proudly earned his Doctor of Divinity from McKinley Theological

Seminary. Dr. Miller is a member of the National Baptist Convention USA and the General Missionary Baptist State Convention of Mississippi, Inc., where he served on the Board of Directors. He served as the First Vice Moderator for the Hope Springs District Association for eight years, as the Moderator of the Counties of MS Baptist District Association (COMBDA) for six years, and as the President of the Metropolitan Ministerial Fellowship for six years. He is a former member of the United Christian Institute and the Rocky Hill Women Institute. He led an International Mission Africa Team, ministering in Lilongwe, Malawi, and surrounding areas, and traveled with pastors and ministers to Israel on a mission trip. Dr. Miller humbly served on the executive committee for Working Together Jackson, a community organization helping Jackson and the surrounding area. He served as the Chaplain for Precinct 3 in Jackson, MS, and was the former President of Ministers for Adoption-Mississippi Children's Home. He was also awarded the E.W. Banks, Sr. Humanitarian Award in 1992, named an honorary member of the Heritage Registry of Who's Who from 2006-2007, and received the Rev. Dr. S.L. Spann Award in 2007, among others. Dr. Miller has been married for 59 years to Mrs. Easter R. Miller, and they have seven daughters: Martha, Anita, Marie, Sandra, Charlene, Elizabeth, and Cynthia.

Introduction

During the five years of trials that my Dad endured, I saw just how strong a man he was then and still is today. He took a stand against sin, and with God's guidance, he never allowed the enemy to make him give up. This was a difficult time for me because the people who were fighting against him were my cousins, with whom I grew up. How could family be so cruel? It took me a long time to get over it and to forgive them for how they treated him. If it hadn't been for God using my Dad to show love despite being hated, to forgive the unforgivable, and to restrain from retaliation, things would have ended badly. I thank God for giving him the faith, strength, and discipline to endure such a difficult time. He taught me to never allow the enemy to make you give up or give in to his schemes.

-Marie Tate

During the five-year trials, I vividly remember almost everything that occurred. I remember my father always saying the Lord told him to stand. I saw my father stand fearlessly, regardless of what they said or tried to do to him. We often call him Jesus' brother. While in the 7th grade, I remember going to school one day and literally having a breakdown at school. I was crying uncontrollably and had to leave class. The assistant principal, who was a minister, encouraged me that it would be okay. After several other experiences at the church, fear set in, and I was literally scared of the people who were against my father. I could not understand why they hated him. I realized when I got older that it was the evil spirits, not the people. I have encountered some of those same spirits in my adult life, but now I know that I have power over them. I am no longer scared because if God is for me, who can be against me?

-Elizabeth Miller-Brister

My experience with the church battles I faced was very difficult as a teenager. I saw and heard a lot of things during this time that were not godly. I remember a time when it got so bad that we had to trail each other to church in our cars. My little sister said to me, 'I don't want to die.' I told her if we are going to die, we will die in the name of Jesus. At that moment, I had to show my little sister courage. As I got older, I realized that people loved the church building, not God. I watched my dad, who is my pastor, show so much love, grace, and compassion to the people who gave him all the trouble. In this battle, my dad taught me how to stand on truth even if you must stand alone. I've learned that if you have God on your side, you can do all things through Christ, who strengthens you. This battle made me the woman that I am today, and I thank God for the trials and tribulations in my life.

-Charlene Miller-Nichols

My experience of the five-year turmoil at New Hope Grove was an experience that helped shape me into the woman I am today. I learned so much from my father as he trusted God and stood on the Word of God through every step of the process. There were times when I asked him when he was going to walk away. He would reply, 'This is the Lord's work, and I will never walk away.' The worst part of the situation was that it involved my mother's family, with whom she spent her childhood. It amazed me that there was so much resistance because my dad stood on what was right, according to the Word of God. It was very challenging for me, because I was engaged to be married and then got married during the turmoil. Usually, when you get married, you join your husband's church. However, I felt compelled to stay and support my dad until things were settled. My husband was very supportive but had no idea what he was getting into. He stood by my family and me throughout the entire process. I will forever be grateful for his love and support during that very trying time. This experience taught me that if you stand on the truth and trust God, He will bring you through any situation. It brought me and my sisters closer, and we stood united with our parents. My mother was a source of comfort for us all during that time. When we did not understand why things were happening the way they were, she often encouraged us to trust God and that things would work out. My faith was strengthened, and my love for God grew strong during the process. I would not want to repeat the process again, but I am thankful for all the lessons that molded me into who I am today.

-Sandra Cotton

Beloved, think it not strange concerning the fiery trial, which is to try you, as though some strange thing happened unto you:

But rejoice, inasmuch as ye are partakers of Christ's sufferings; that, when his glory shall be revealed, ye may be glad also with exceeding joy.

1 Peter: 12-13

Don't Misunderstand THE MISSION Of God's Word

The Key to Success
in Ministry & Life

DR. CHARLES D. MILLER

Don't Misunderstand the Mission & the Mystery of God's Power

Don't misunderstand the mission nor the mystery of God when you start your journey for the Lord. The reason I am writing this book is because God took me through an unusual journey. Unknowingly, my preparation started during a very difficult time as a supervisor at the Jackson Country Club. While employed there for 14 years I learned to be bold, speak the truth to those in authority and defend people who were treated wrongly. God eventually led me to leave the Jackson Country Club and open two small convenience stores. I owned the first store for 12 years and the second store for 8 years. The income from the stores allowed me to support my family for about 2 years. I was also able to support my family by buying and selling cows and hogs.

I was a member of the Craftsman Club for a few years before I eventually became the manager. We organized horse races, poker games and card gambling on the weekends. We also hosted fish fries and beer parties that sometimes went on until 4:00 in the morning. One Saturday God came to me and told me to leave the Craftsman Club. The next day I went to church and after the service while on my way home, God told me not to go back to the club. When I got home, I locked myself in my bedroom and wrote out my resignation. God told me to give it to someone who would not question me about it. I turned in my letter of resignation and from that day forward, I never returned to another club. One Sunday, two of my daughters were getting baptized and while sitting in church, the Holy Spirit came over me and picked me up. When I came to myself, I was sitting in the chair. That was the day I gave my life to Christ Jesus. I have never missed church since that day unless I was out of the country.

After two years, I started looking for another job. After searching for quite a while, I sent out an application for a job and received a call for an interview. The interview was scheduled for 3:00 p.m. The day of the interview I was sleeping and would have missed the interview, but God woke me up at 2:45 p.m. and I made it there at 2:55 p.m.

After the general manager interviewed me, I told him I did not think he could pay me enough to take the job due to the amount of money I made at the Jackson Country Club, and I told him that the job must be from 8 a.m. to 5 p.m. He agreed to give me those hours and hired me as an assistant supervisor. God had started preparing me to be a pastor, but about three months after I began working there I started to have problems with my Caucasian co-workers. They were determined to get me fired but God was teaching me to have staying power. They kept trying to sabotage me by wrecking my workplace when I would leave for lunch. I reported it, but all three of my co-workers denied it. God was also teaching me patience, and it went on for years. I told them that God gave me that job and no one could make me leave. They conspired with the personnel manager and all four of them said they were going to get rid of me. One day I was going up the escalator and my co-workers were coming down, but they did not see me. I overheard them say that they were going to get rid of me. God will always show you your enemies, but you have to be connected to Him.

Their determination to get rid of me increased, so I intensified my staying power by going to the Equal Opportunity Office. I relied on God and He guided me step by step. The officer told me to write everything down for six months and then call back. He warned me that they were going to get rid of me, and I said, "That's what you think." So, I began to record everything and after those six months, I called the office again and met with a lawyer. I asked her to write a letter to the general manager and the personnel manager, telling them to fire the young man who was giving me so much trouble. The letter stated if they did not fire him, I would sue them for $250,000. She wrote the letter and sent it to them. On that Monday morning, the personnel manager called me to his office and said, "You know I can fire you?" I replied, "Yes, but if you do, I'm going to sue for $250,000." I told him I thought he had not been used to being around Black people, but I found out he was just prejudice. I told him they were going to fire him and he said it would never happen because I was Black. He did not know that God woke me up and sent me to that job. They soon fired the employees who were giving me problems along with the personnel manager. Everyone else involved quit. After they were fired, I was promoted and given an office. While dealing with all the issues on my job, I was still faithful in church and the Lord continued preparing me for the journey.

As the journey continued God began to show me problems at the church. The former pastor had asked to have his salary raised by $25 at the church business meeting and the members acted out so badly. The argument got so heated that the business meeting had to be dismissed. It was such a bad experience and it taught me that you can be in the church, but not have the church in you. In other words, you can be in the church building for years but can still be unsaved. This was one of my first experiences seeing so called Christians acting ungodly in the church. As my commitment got stronger with God, He allowed me to join the male choir, become a Sunday School teacher, and then a deacon. Our male choir went to many churches over the years and the spirit would dwell with me as we ministered in song. Then it came to me that I had to preach, but I wasn't sure. I refused to preach because I wanted to make sure it was God calling me. I began losing weight and many thought I was sick, but I was just waiting for God to speak to me. When my uncle who was a pastor passed away, I attended his funeral. I was sitting in the church when God spoke to me three times, saying, "Preach, Preach, Preach." I asked the person next to me if they heard the voice, but no one did except me. Another time I remember leaning on a tree outside one day at home. I had begun to fall, then a cool breeze blew. I said, "Lord, don't let me fall..." and He picked me up. Those standing around said, "You almost fell and we couldn't get to you." They took me inside and laid me on a bed. I slept for a while and when I got up, I still refused to say I would preach. Something came over me, and I could not shake it.

I went to my pastor and told him that I needed to talk to him, but I didn't know what I was going to say. One Sunday evening he closed the church door and started backing up in the middle of the church and asked me what was on my mind. When I opened my mouth, I said to him, "I have to preach." He said he already knew it. My journey continued and God wanted me to start observing everything. I noticed that 98% of the people didn't act like they were saved. When I began to go deeper into scripture, I then understood what God required of His people and I realized it was not happening at the church. At a business meeting one night, our pastor gave his resignation letter. I was late getting to the meeting, but when I got there, the pastor told me he had resigned. Then, an older lady ran up to me and said, "You will be our next pastor." After observing the church for a period of time, I personally did not want to be the pastor there. I wanted to pastor somewhere else and I did not ask to be considered. The church selected a pulpit committee. Pastors came from everywhere. They made me the pulpit supplier, meaning if no preacher showed up, then I would preach.

This went on for years. At the time, we had an "Amen corner." Most Sundays, the church would have plenty of preachers to preach. One of the committee members said they were going to put my name in the running for pastor, but the deacons at the church did not want me as their pastor. The oldest deacon called a vote at the meeting. God said to me that He placed me there to clean up the church. Before they voted me in, the church was full-time. Then they voted full-time out and voted on three preachers to be Pastor, including me. They called my name first and I got 85% of the church's votes. So, I began the work. When we started to have Bible class, no one came except me and my family and this went on for months. I remember one night; it was thundering and lightning and the wind was blowing. My wife said, "Ain't nobody coming out here." Then, the very next Wednesday night, God sent about 16 people and they have been coming ever since. As I continued on my journey, I pastored and sang in the male choir. Some people started forgetting that the church belonged to God. They forgot that God said, "…Upon this rock, I will build my church; and the gates of hell shall not prevail against it." (Matthew 16:18) Most people don't realize that when they are fighting against the church, they are fighting against God and they can't win. All God wants is someone to stand. The people told me they would run me off. I told them that God sent me there and they could not run me off. They began to plot against me or so they thought, but they were actually plotting against God. For five years, they fought against me. God prepared me for the mission and I had to realize the mission belonged to God. He wants to use us as His instrument to do things pleasing to Him.

So, the first thing you must do is recognize that you must prepare for the work of God. You must get your direction from God and His direction comes from His Word. Then, you must be able to hear the voice of God. As you move step by step on this journey, you must make sure that you are following the direction of God and not your own direction. When God led me out of the world and empowered me to do this ministry, the first thing I had to make sure of was that it was not my mission. I had to make sure that I knew it was God's mission and that He was using me as a vessel. We must pray and never get in a hurry, and you must wait on the voice of God until He speaks to your spirit. Once you do that, you can do exactly what He wants you to do.

If you ever get into "self," you will never be successful in the mission. The enemy is always trying to intervene and mess your mind up because his goal is to keep you off the mission.

#1 You must make sure that you are humble and under the mighty hand of God.

Don't let anyone cause you to lose your temper or bear ill will towards an individual. The mission that God placed in my spirit is to be able to help others move forward in who God wants them to be. As we were going through our mission, we faced all kinds of interference from the enemy. The devil tried his best to cause me to get out of character. As a matter of fact, not only did I stay in character, but I also made sure that everyone around me stayed in character. I wanted to make sure that they did not allow the enemy to take them off track. If the enemy takes you off track, you will fail. When the devil gets in you and gets you off track, you will act out of character and you can never let that happen.

We had 14 days of prayer to strengthen us during the mission. We went from house-to-house like it was done in the old days. We prayed, God slayed people in the spirit, and the Holy Spirit filled the houses. We did this for 14 days straight because the enemy had come against us so strongly. God was directing us although we were doing ministry from house to house.

#2 God will give you directions on what to do and how to do it.

God gave us direction on what to do and how to do the things we needed to get done. He directed us on how to stay safe from the enemy and protected us as long as we relied on Him. When I was going through the mission, I had some people around me who wanted to take revenge. I said, "NO WAY...NO WAY!" I began to think about how we could be successful on this mission. I also thought about how would others see Jesus in us if I allowed us to get out of character and do something that was not according to the Word of God. If you are reading this book you should understand that when God gives you a mission, it's not about your own agenda. You are just a vessel being used by

God. To succeed in the mission, you must always have a prayer life and a forgiving heart. You can't harbor anything in your heart against anyone. No matter how badly people treat you or how they come at you. You must hold your peace and let God fight your battles. If you do this you will always be successful. After Jesus came to Earth, died, and rose again, we were given the power to stand. God promised that He would fight for us if we don't get in the way.

As the journey continued, we understood that we had to carry ourselves according to the Word of God and He kept giving us direction through His Word. You must prepare yourself with the Word of God and ask Him to show you how to walk. Let God open you up so that you may understand His will. This is actually what God did. When God sent His son to Earth, He was and is our first example. If we follow His example, we will never be defeated. He told each of us that if He is with us, He is more than the whole world against us.

We have another promise, Hebrews 13:5 which says, "I will never leave thee, nor forsake thee." We can walk away from

God, but God will never walk away from us if we do His will. Every time the enemy tried to stop or block the mission, God would intervene. I have always encouraged people about the importance of praying and asking God to surround you. God honored my prayer and put the right people around us to help. Just like when God sent Moses to Egypt...He put people around him like Aaron, to deliver the people. Our ultimate purpose is to help deliver people out of their sins so when Jesus comes back, they will be ready to go to Heaven with Him. If people realized why the church was established, which most people don't, they would understand that the church was established to be a light in this dark world. When men get sick and tired of themselves, they can come to Christ and live a free life in this world. Jesus makes it very clear that whom He makes free is free indeed.

According to Luke 9:23, Jesus said, if anyone would come after me, let him deny himself, take up his cross, and follow me daily. I think people go to church just to have a good time, but the only way you can have a good time is with the Holy Spirit. We're supposed to be in church to worship God for all He has done and does for us every day. Our ultimate goal is to worship and praise Him and give Him glory for what He has done. The reason the Lord led me to write this book was so that others can really understand and know how you can go through all kinds of ridicule, be shot at, cursed out, and see how people can put their finger in your face and call you everything but a child of God; And what do you do? You look at them, smile and say to yourself, "God's gonna get them." You do not have to worry about your life.

One reason I'm so stern about this and why I say you have to prepare yourself with the Word of God is because of the story of Job. When God and satan had a conversation about Job, who lived a perfect life, satan asked God why he couldn't get to him. It was because God had a hedge around Job. But God asked him, "Have you considered my servant Job?" Satan said no because God had placed a protective hedge around him, but God told Satan that He would remove the hedge. God lets us know through His Word that Satan can't do anything to you unless He allows him to. Satan attacked Job, but God told him not to mess with his soul. The same way we were on the mission, we had to understand that if we lived according to God's Word, followed His direction, and obeyed His voice, our mission would be successful. God will save us so that we can be a light in this dark world. Don't be afraid to speak the truth and never compromise the gospel of Jesus Christ. I always say that we must become imitators of the Word so we will be successful. Although I faced many challenges, that is why I was victorious in everything I did.

I experienced some very dark times with the people as I was building this ministry. They even shut the church down and threatened me for five years but because I was following the steps of God and Jesus Christ, we came out victorious. Although the enemy attacked the church, it was not destroyed. God has blessed us far beyond measure. The church I pastor has been there for 177 years. When I came, it had been standing for 135 years. God blessed me just like He blessed Job; He gave me double for my trouble. It does not matter what anyone says, people must follow the footsteps of Jesus and obey Him to the best of their ability. You must keep your focus on the prize, which is Heaven. I promise you, God will always be with you and will take you all the way through.

A lady came to me, spoke into my life, and essentially repeated to me everything I went through. She looked at me and told me that God was going to send me overseas to do ministry. I had no idea that 10 years later, I would go on a mission trip to Africa. I went all over the villages, ministering to the people and preaching. People were being saved and slain in the spirit and demons went running. God will send you where you need to be. He also sent me to Israel to do mission work.

So, what I am saying is that each of you have an opportunity to be used. God wants to use us for His glory. If God does not get the glory out of our lives, the devil will try his best to get it. I have nothing for the devil because all I have is for the Lord. I try to encourage people all the time. I always ask the church, "Why would you want to follow somebody that you already know wants to kill you, and why wouldn't you want to follow somebody that wants you to have an abundant life?" According to John 10:10 "The thief cometh not, but for to steal, and to kill, and to destroy: I am come that they might have life, and that they might have it more abundantly." My mission for this book is to make sure that people understand that they can stand and do anything that God has commissioned them to do. They must follow the direction of God, obey God, seek God, and hear His voice, then He will set them on the right path. According to Matthew 6:33, "But seek ye first the kingdom of God, and his righteousness, and all these things shall be added unto you."

People really don't know how to be blessed. God does not mind if you have material things. He just wants you to recognize Him and put Him first. If you put Him first, God will bless you abundantly. My mission is to open the eyes of someone. Since I have been through this ordeal, I have been to many conventions and met many pastors. I have shared with them what I went through and they were blessed and encouraged. They told me that they were going back home "to pastor." Basically, I told them that God called you to pastor and made you the overseer. You must lead the people to where God wants them to be, not where you as the pastor, want them to be. Always know that God did not call you to do your own thing. He gave us a message and a mission. We must make sure we follow it as directly as possible and according to His will. You all need to know that God is still raising up people just like He did in olden times. He raised up Moses. He raised up Daniel. He raised up Isaiah. He spoke to all of these prophets and sent them on a mission. Their mission was to make sure that the world knew who God was and is. I want to let everyone know that God is an Almighty God! He sent Jesus to bring all of us back to Him. God wants us all to understand that He does the work and uses us as vessels. We don't do the work. The only way for you to stay humble is to realize that you are not doing the work, but you are only being used, led, and guided by the Holy Spirit. God is doing it for His glory and for His honor. God will open doors for you that you never thought would open and take you places you never thought you would go. He will do things for you that you never thought He would do. God is still in the blessing business.

I am 83 years old and I have never spent a night in the hospital. I do not have rheumatism or any headaches. People ask me how I can get around like I'm 45 years old and I say, listen….. let me share this with you..."I was an old man when I was a sinner, but when I became saved, I became a new creature." I then say, "You've never read anywhere in the Bible where the Holy Spirit was old."

What God does is keep us energized because we must understand, He is our life. We would be nothing apart from Him. As a matter of fact, I have been pastoring for 40 years. In those 40 years, I've never missed a Sunday unless I was out of the country. We have enrichment classes on Tuesday nights, Bible class on Wednesday nights and two worship services on Sundays. We do not have a large congregation, but I promised God that I would be faithful unto death. The name of our church is New Birth Fellowship M.B. Church. I always tell New Birth that I will preach to those I see. Jeremiah had a problem and was mad because the people would not hear him. God told him that they weren't going to hear him, but he charged him to preach anyway. He told him that his job was to tell the people what He said and He would take care of the people. God took them into captivity for 70 years. After 70 years, God allowed them to return to their homeland. Just like Jeremiah was charged to preach to the people when they did not want to hear him, pastors are charged to preach to the people today. Pastors must preach in season and out of season. In other words, they must preach when the people want to hear them and when they don't want to hear them. I think we get mixed up on our mission because we think one thing, but God has a remedy and a mission for the church. Through our social media platform, my outreach ministry reaches places like Pakistan and Africa. People tune in every Sunday. I may not have a large congregation, but people from all over the world call and tune in to my ministry every Sunday morning and Wednesday night. I tell people that technology is not bad. A lot of people think technology is bad, but God has made it possible for me to sit right here in Jackson, Mississippi and still reach people all over the world. Of course, a lot of people use technology for the wrong reasons, but God has allowed me to use it for ministry. This is what we must understand that everything God has made is good. The devil takes things and makes it bad and when this happens, we take the wrong mission and follow the enemy instead of following God. Everything that was made on the earth was made for a purpose. This is what we must understand, we must be able to distinguish the will of God for our lives and what God has done in our lives. You see, God loves us. We are the only beings that God made for Himself. We must praise Him because He made us to glorify Him. He made us to be a light unto this world and to carry the message to the whole world. God raised up a nation called Egypt. At that time, it was the strongest nation in the world. Then, He got a smaller nation, Israel, who stayed in Egypt for 400 years. God used them to show His power and then He sent Moses and Aaron to deliver them.

God wants everyone to know He is in charge of everything and whatever God decides to do, nobody can stop it. If you are with Him, you must follow Him, obey Him and love Him unconditionally. You must be faithful because the Bible teaches us to be faithful unto Him and be found faithful. A lot of people do what they want and that is not right. We must make sure we are following God's word to the 'T'. You can't just say, you're going to do whatever you want to do. If God says do it, you must do it to the best of your ability.

The Holy Spirit will lead, guide, and keep you. The Holy Spirit is the one that teaches us. Gods says that the Holy Spirit will teach you and lead you in all things. When He sent His disciples out, He told them that when they go out, do not try to remember anything. He told them when they went out to open their mouths, He would speak through them. People do not realize that if there is nothing in you, nothing will come out of you. When God saved me, I searched the Word of God for five years. I was tutored by spiritual people, who understood the Word of God and I received their teachings. Everyone must sit at someone's feet to be taught and be empowered by the Holy Spirit. When we go on missions, we must realize that these are not our missions. Another thing is you must love everyone, no matter who they are, what they do to you or how they treat you.

You must love them unconditionally. I realized one thing in my life and that is when a person is truly saved, they will not fight against you. The only reason people fight against you is when they don't know Jesus. The Holy Spirit is not going to fight against Holy Spirit, but evil spirits will fight against the Holy Spirit. According to Matthew 16:18, Jesus said, "Upon this rock I will build my church; and the gates of hell shall not prevail against it." It doesn't matter what comes up against you, it will never win. You must always understand that no matter what you are going through or how it looks, with God you will win. In fact, I have seen things that look bad, but in my spirit, I knew that I had victory because God sent me on the mission. He had already told me that He was going to tear the church all the way down because the foundation was messed up. God was not talking about the building but about the people. They were messed up. They were drinking, smoking, and doing everything under the sun, but God sent me there for a purpose. I was there to clean His house up and to set the church up on a solid, spiritual foundation. That is where we are now. New Birth, the church that I pastor, is on a solid spiritual foundation. Everyone there is not saved, but I am charged to love them and help them. There is a diverse group of people in the church. If everyone was saved, you would not need a preacher.

As a pastor, you must understand God's mission and the people He has placed you over. You must understand how to be true to the mission and how to give the right message so that the people can become better. Even if the people do not change, you still must deliver the message. This is my mission and it will be the mission until I die. I tell people that God is going to be first in my life as long as I live.

Amen.

A lot of pastors talk about retiring, but I can't find anywhere in the Bible where God says a preacher should retire. I prayed before writing this book and the Lord told me what I needed to say. This book is fully inspired by God. I belong to Him and if God can't use me for His glory, then all my work is in vain. If I'm not doing the will of God and if the Holy Spirit is not leading me, what am I doing? I always tell people that when God saves you, even the devil knows you're saved. Everyone is going to know you are saved. If no one knows you are saved but you, then you are not saved. According Acts 19:15, "And the evil spirit answered and said, Jesus I know, and Paul I know; but who are ye?" If you aren't saved, you can't go on pretending you know something that you don't know. You must be real when you are going on your mission. When I was in Africa, demons came out at me while I was laying hands on people. They were passing out and getting healed. Demons appeared in the crowd, but I didn't say anything. When I turned and looked at them, they took off running. The Holy Spirit will put fear in people if you have God in you, and according to Acts 1:8: "But ye shall receive power, after that the Holy Ghost is come upon you..." God gives us power for the mission. You can't do this mission if you don't have the power of the Holy Spirit. My mission is to always please God. I tell the church I am going to love the people, but I am going to obey God. You must love people and people must know you love them regardless of how they feel or think about you. You must love them unconditionally, but you must obey God. Some people try to be people pleasers, not me. I am a God-pleaser. My mission is to please God every day of my life and love people unconditionally. If the preacher ain't right, then the church ain't going to be right. Most pastors that I have talked to will say, "I will be there as long as the people want me there." I look at them and say, "What did you say? How can you say that?" Pastors need to know if God places them, no man can move them. Pastors also must understand the mission because if they don't understand the mission and focus on the people, they will miss the mission that God has sent them on. God will send the pastor as a lamb among wolves. The mission is to make disciples along the way, and everything that comes against you on the mission is for your good. There are three things that I tell people all the time that they MUST know before starting the mission.

The three things you MUST know are:

1. You MUST know you are saved without any doubt.

2. You MUST know that you were called to preach by God.
3. If you are going to pastor a church, you MUST know that you were placed there by God.

I've had people offer me opportunities to pastor, tell me that they have 500 members and all I have to do is this or that... No, I'm not going into any church unless the Lord sends me. You can't help people if the Lord does not send you. When a pastor is placed at a church, you can't be fearful of anyone. God said to fear no man and to fear Him only. Even with all of this, you must love people. I have been ridiculed and talked about. I tell people to remember one thing, they did the same thing to Jesus. Jesus always forgave them because they did not know what they were doing. Remember, we must have a forgiving spirit. People need the Lord, but they are outside of His will. Many are not concerned for the people, but we need to be because we must do it God's way and not our way because our plans and ways will not work. A lot of people don't want to hear that, but it is true. When people get saved, they become faithful, obedient, and loving. You will know because what comes from one heart will be received by another heart. We will connect in the spirit because we are one body in Christ. If you are saved and your spirit is right, it will go from heart to heart. The Holy Spirit is what makes us one. How can two agree unless they walk together? We must understand and realize that when you are around unsaved people, you still must love them. The goal is to show love because people need to see the Jesus in you. The church is a witness for Christ and a witness to the Word of God. After you become saved, the Word of God will build you up so that when you go back out into the world, you will be able to stand against all the things that come against you. You will be tried on every side but if you stand, God will stand with you. This journey will not be hard if you follow God's plan because He will give you the type of peace that surpasses all understanding and you must believe it with your whole heart. If you keep the faith, God's power will override satan's influence.

This is my mission.

Made in the USA
Columbia, SC
29 January 2024